Lessons on Demand Presents

Student Workbook for The Girl Who Drank the Moon

By:

John Pennington

Cover Image by:

Pixabay Creative Commons

The lessons on demand series is designed to provide ready to use resources for novel study. In this book you will find key vocabulary, student organizer pages, and assessments. This guide is the Student Workbook. The Teachers Guide will have answers and an open layout of the activities. The Student Workbook can be used alone but it will not include answers.

Look for bound print Teacher Editions on Amazon.com

PDF versions can be found on Teacherspayteachers.com

Vocabulary Box

Definition:

Draw:

Kohl

Related words:

Use in a sentence:

Definition:

Draw:

Inexplicable

Related words:

Use in a sentence:

Vocabulary Box

Definition:

Draw:

Façade

Related words:

Use in a sentence:

Definition:

Draw:

Contemplation

Related words:

Use in a sentence:

Vocabulary Box

Definition:

Draw:

Hobbled

Related words:

Use in a sentence:

Definition:

Draw:

Luminous

Related words:

Use in a sentence:

Vocabulary Box

Definition:

Draw:

Swale

Related words:

Use in a sentence:

Definition:

Draw:

Subdued

Related words:

Use in a sentence:

Vocabulary Box

Definition:

Draw:

Millennia

Related words:

Use in a sentence:

Definition:

Draw:

Aghast

Related words:

Use in a sentence:

Vocabulary Box

Definition:

Draw:

Pontifications

Related words:

Use in a sentence:

Definition:

Draw:

Clabbering

Related words:

Use in a sentence:

Create the Test

Question: Who lives in the woods that the people in the Protectorate are afraid of?

Answer:

Question: What do the people of the protectorate do on the Day of Sacrifice?

Answer:

Question: Following the Day of Sacrifice for the Protectorate the Free Cities get what holiday?

Answer:

Question: What name does Xan give the child she decides to keep?

Answer:

NAME:

TEACHER:

Date:

Assignment: Distinguish how life is different for the Protectorate and The Free Cities.

NAME:

TEACHER:

Date:

Character Sketch

Gherland

Draw a picture

Personality/ Distinguishing marks

Connections to other characters

Important Actions

NAME:

TEACHER:

Date:

Character Sketch

Xan

Personality/ Distinguishing marks

Draw a picture

Connections to other characters

Important Actions

NAME:

TEACHER:

Date:

Research connections

What am I researching? Volcano

Source (URL, Book, Magazine, Interview)

Facts I found that could be useful or notes

1.

2.

3.

4.

5.

6.

NAME:

TEACHER:

Date:

Assignment: Pyramid

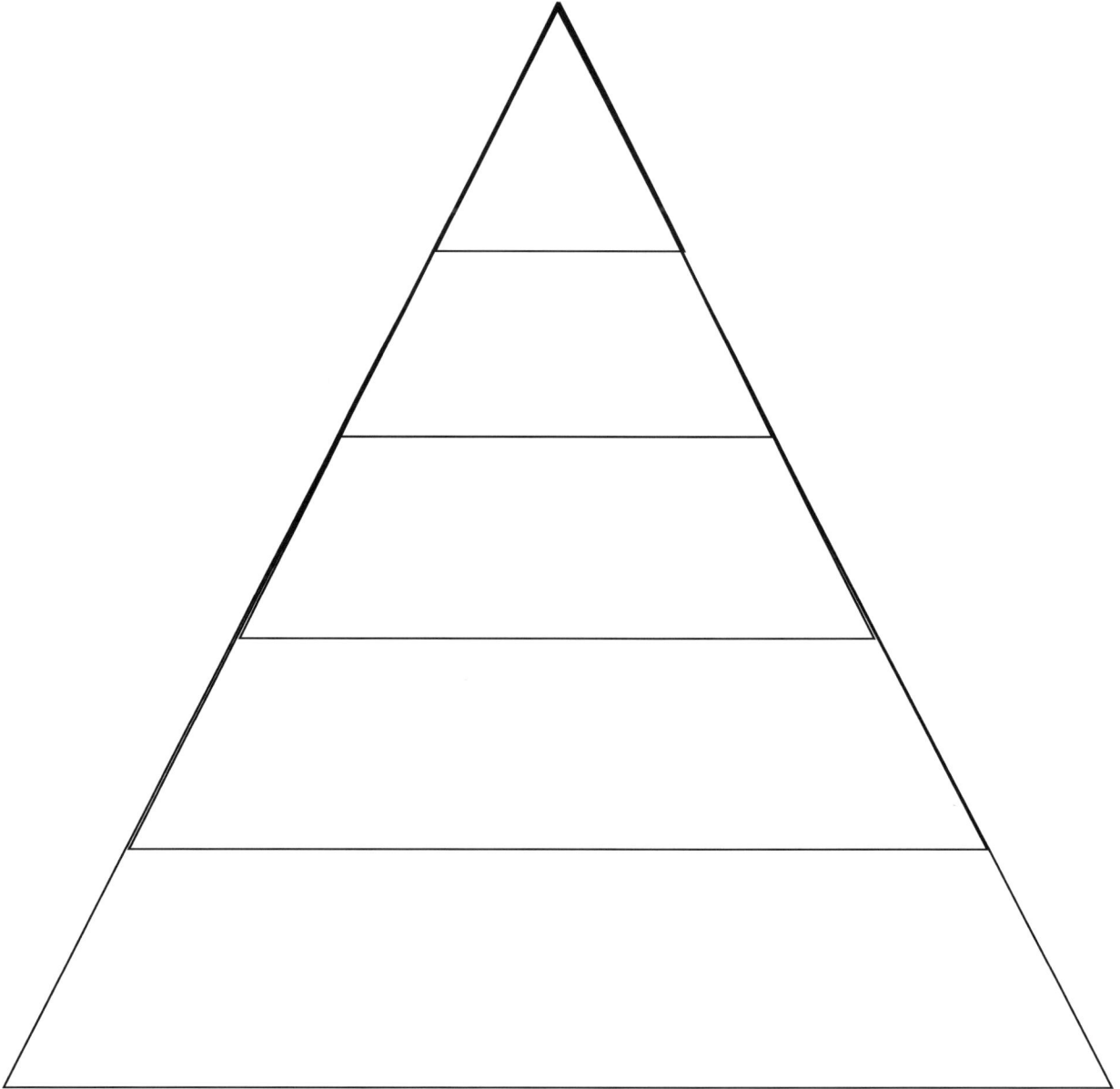

NAME:

TEACHER:

Date:

Assignment: <u>Discussion Questions</u>

Do you think any of the characters mentioned are villains? Why?

Why did Xan not take the baby to the free cities?

Why do the Elder continue the story of the witch in the bog?

NAME:

TEACHER:

Date:

Vocabulary Box

Definition:

Draw:

Hypocrisy

Related words:

Use in a sentence:

Definition:

Draw:

Admonished

Related words:

Use in a sentence:

Vocabulary Box

Definition:

Draw:

Inconsequential

Related words:

Use in a sentence:

Definition:

Draw:

Convalesced

Related words:

Use in a sentence:

Vocabulary Box

Definition:

Draw:

Inert

Related words:

Use in a sentence:

Definition:

Draw:

Akimbo

Related words:

Use in a sentence:

Vocabulary Box

Definition:

Draw:

Stasis

Related words:

Use in a sentence:

Definition:

Draw:

Obscure

Related words:

Use in a sentence:

Vocabulary Box

Definition:

Draw:

Lament

Related words:

Use in a sentence:

Definition:

Draw:

Decoupage

Related words:

Use in a sentence:

NAME:

TEACHER:

Date:

Vocabulary Box

Definition:

Draw:

Rapport

Related words:

Use in a sentence:

Definition:

Draw:

Proliferation

Related words:

Use in a sentence:

Create the Test

Question: Why is Xan worried about Luna growing up?

Answer:

Question: Why is Antain going to be in trouble with the elders?

Answer:

Question: Once Luna starts using magic what begins to happen to Xan?

Answer:

Question: Who does Antain visit in the tower?

Answer:

NAME:

TEACHER:

Date:

Assignment: You have one day of magical powers like Luna. What do you do with your day? Name a minimum of 10 things you would change and why you would change them.

Character Sketch

Antain

Personality/ Distinguishing marks

Draw a picture

Connections to other characters

Important Actions

NAME:

TEACHER:

Date:

Character Sketch

Grelk

Personality/ Distinguishing marks

Draw a picture

Connections to other characters

Important Actions

Character Sketch

Fryian

Personality/ Distinguishing marks

Draw a picture

Connections to other characters

Important Actions

NAME:

TEACHER:

Date:

Advertisement: Draw an advertisement for the Protectorate

NAME: TEACHER:

Date:

Precognition Sheet

Who ?

What's going to happen?

What will be the result?

Who ?

What's going to happen?

What will be the result?

Who ?

What's going to happen?

What will be the result?

Who ?

What's going to happen?

What will be the result?

How many did you get correct?

1.

2.

3.

4.

5.

Sequencing or timeline

Assignment: <u>Discussion Question</u>

Was Xan right in putting Luna to sleep?

Why was Antain having a hard time in the Protectorate even though he is a very agreeable person?

Vocabulary Box

Definition:

Draw:

Prodigious

Related words:

Use in a sentence:

Definition:

Draw:

Trance

Related words:

Use in a sentence:

Vocabulary Box

Definition:

Draw:

Retrospect

Related words:

Use in a sentence:

Definition:

Draw:

Fiasco

Related words:

Use in a sentence:

Vocabulary Box

Definition:

Draw:

Chastised

Related words:

Use in a sentence:

Definition:

Draw:

Gravitas

Related words:

Use in a sentence:

Vocabulary Box

Definition:

Draw:

Peevish

Related words:

Use in a sentence:

Definition:

Draw:

Apothecary

Related words:

Use in a sentence:

NAME:

Vocabulary Box

Definition:

Draw:

Tenacious

Related words:

Use in a sentence:

Definition:

Draw:

Belligerent

Related words:

Use in a sentence:

Vocabulary Box

Definition:

Draw:

Unorthodox

Related words:

Use in a sentence:

Definition:

Draw:

Benevolent

Related words:

Use in a sentence:

Test

Question: What was Luna no longer able to hear?

Answer:

Question: What profession does Antain pursue once he leaves the elders?

Answer:

Question: What magical item does Fyrian retrieve?

Answer:

Question: What does Antain plan to do to save his baby?

Answer:

NAME:

TEACHER:

Date:

Assignment: Draw what you think a map of the area should look like. Include all the locations mentioned in the story.

Character Sketch

Luna

Personality/ Distinguishing marks

Draw a picture

Connections to other characters

Important Actions

NAME:

TEACHER:

Date:

Character Sketch

Sister Ignatia

Personality/ Distinguishing marks

Connections to other characters

Draw a picture

Important Actions

Chapter to Poem

Assignment: Select 20 words found in the chapter to create a poem where each line is 3 words long.

Title:

_____   _____   _____

_____   _____   _____

_____   _____   _____

_____   _____   _____

_____   _____   _____

NAME:

TEACHER:

Date:

Draw the Scene: What five things have you included in the scene?

1   2   3

4   5

NAME:

TEACHER:

Date:

Precognition Sheet

Who ?

What's going to happen?

What will be the result?

Who ?

What's going to happen?

What will be the result?

Who ?

What's going to happen?

What will be the result?

Who ?

What's going to happen?

What will be the result?

How many did you get correct?

NAME:

TEACHER:

Date:

Who, What, When, Where, and How

Who

What

Where

When

How

NAME:

TEACHER:

Date:

Assignment: <u>Discussion Questions</u>

How does Antain transform during the story?

What do you think has been forgotten by different characters?

Vocabulary Box

Definition:

Draw:

Dissuade

Related words:

Use in a sentence:

Definition:

Draw:

Gaunt

Related words:

Use in a sentence:

Vocabulary Box

Definition:

Draw:

Anecdotal

Related words:

Use in a sentence:

Definition:

Draw:

Forensic

Related words:

Use in a sentence:

Vocabulary Box

Definition:

Draw:

Duplicity

Related words:

Use in a sentence:

Definition:

Draw:

Deceit

Related words:

Use in a sentence:

Vocabulary Box

Definition:

Draw:

Evasion

Related words:

Use in a sentence:

Definition:

Draw:

Observatory

Related words:

Use in a sentence:

Vocabulary Box

Definition:

Draw:

Precise

Related words:

Use in a sentence:

Definition:

Draw:

Arabesques

Related words:

Use in a sentence:

Vocabulary Box

Definition:

Draw:

Enumerated

Related words:

Use in a sentence:

Definition:

Draw:

Impervious

Related words:

Use in a sentence:

Test

Question: What has changed about the madwomen?

Answer:

Question: What does Sister Ingitia plan to do to Antain?

Answer:

Question: What item allows Luna to understand magic?

Answer:

Question: What is Sister Ignatia also called?

Answer:

NAME:

TEACHER:

Date:

Assignment: Create a magic item (similar to the Seven League Boots) and develop a back story for your item.

NAME:

TEACHER:

Date:

Character Sketch

Ethyne

Personality/ Distinguishing marks

Draw a picture

Connections to other characters

Important Actions

NAME:

TEACHER:

Date:

Lost Scene: Write a scene that takes place between _____ and
_____

Making Connections

What is the connection?

Hope

1.

2.

3.

4.

5.

Sequencing or timeline

NAME: _____

TEACHER: _____

Date: _____

What would you do?

Character: _____

What did they do?

Example from text:

What would you do?

Why would that be better?

Character: _____

What did they do?

Example from text:

What would you do?

Why would that be better?

Character: _____

What did they do?

Example from text:

What would you do?

Why would that be better?

NAME:

Assignment: <u>Discussion Questions</u>

Was Xan right in locking Luna's magic away?

Could someone like Sister Ignitia exist in the real world?

Vocabulary Box

Definition:

Draw:

Wanderlust

Related words:

Use in a sentence:

Definition:

Draw:

Indolent

Related words:

Use in a sentence:

Vocabulary Box

Definition:

Draw:

Imbued

Related words:

Use in a sentence:

Definition:

Draw:

Copious

Related words:

Use in a sentence:

Vocabulary Box

Definition:

Draw:

Spectrum

Related words:

Use in a sentence:

Definition:

Draw:

Ambulate

Related words:

Use in a sentence:

Vocabulary Box

Definition:

Draw:

Prevision

Related words:

Use in a sentence:

Definition:

Draw:

Chrysalis

Related words:

Use in a sentence:

Vocabulary Box

Definition:

Draw:

Rheumy

Related words:

Use in a sentence:

Definition:

Draw:

Desiccate

Related words:

Use in a sentence:

Vocabulary Box

Definition:

Draw:

Repellant

Related words:

Use in a sentence:

Definition:

Draw:

Implicitly

Related words:

Use in a sentence:

Create the Test

Question: What does Sister Ignitia feed on when she is loosing strength in the woods?

Answer:

Question: What allows Luna to get away from Sister Ignatia?

Answer:

Question: What allows Adara to get away from Sister Ignatia?

Answer:

Question: What happens to Glerk and Xan at the end of the story?

Answer:

NAME:

TEACHER:

Date:

Assignment: Write down all the chapters and why the name is appropriate.

NAME:

TEACHER:

Date:

Character Sketch

Adara

Personality/ Distinguishing marks

Draw a picture

Connections to other characters

Important Actions

NAME:

TEACHER:

Date:

Create the Test

Question:

Answer:

Question:

Answer:

Question:

Answer:

Question:

Answer:

Top Ten List—Events

1.

2.

3.

4.

5.

6.

7.

8.

9.

10.

NAME:

TEACHER:

Date:

Assignment: <u>Discussion Questions</u>

Compare how emotions are used in the story.

What do you think this world will be like in 500 years?

What will Luna do now that she can use magic?

Who are the heroes of the story and what makes them a hero?

NAME:

TEACHER:

Date:

Advertisement: Draw an advertisement for _____

NAME:

TEACHER:

Date:

Chapter to Poem

Assignment: Select 20 words found in the chapter to create a poem where each line is 3 words long.

Title:

_____ _____ _____

_____ _____ _____

_____ _____ _____

_____ _____ _____

_____ _____ _____

NAME:

TEACHER:

Date:

Character Sketch

Name

Draw a picture

Personality/ Distinguishing marks

Connections to other characters

Important Actions

NAME:

TEACHER:

Date:

Comic Strip

NAME:

TEACHER:

Date:

Compare and Contrast

Venn Diagram

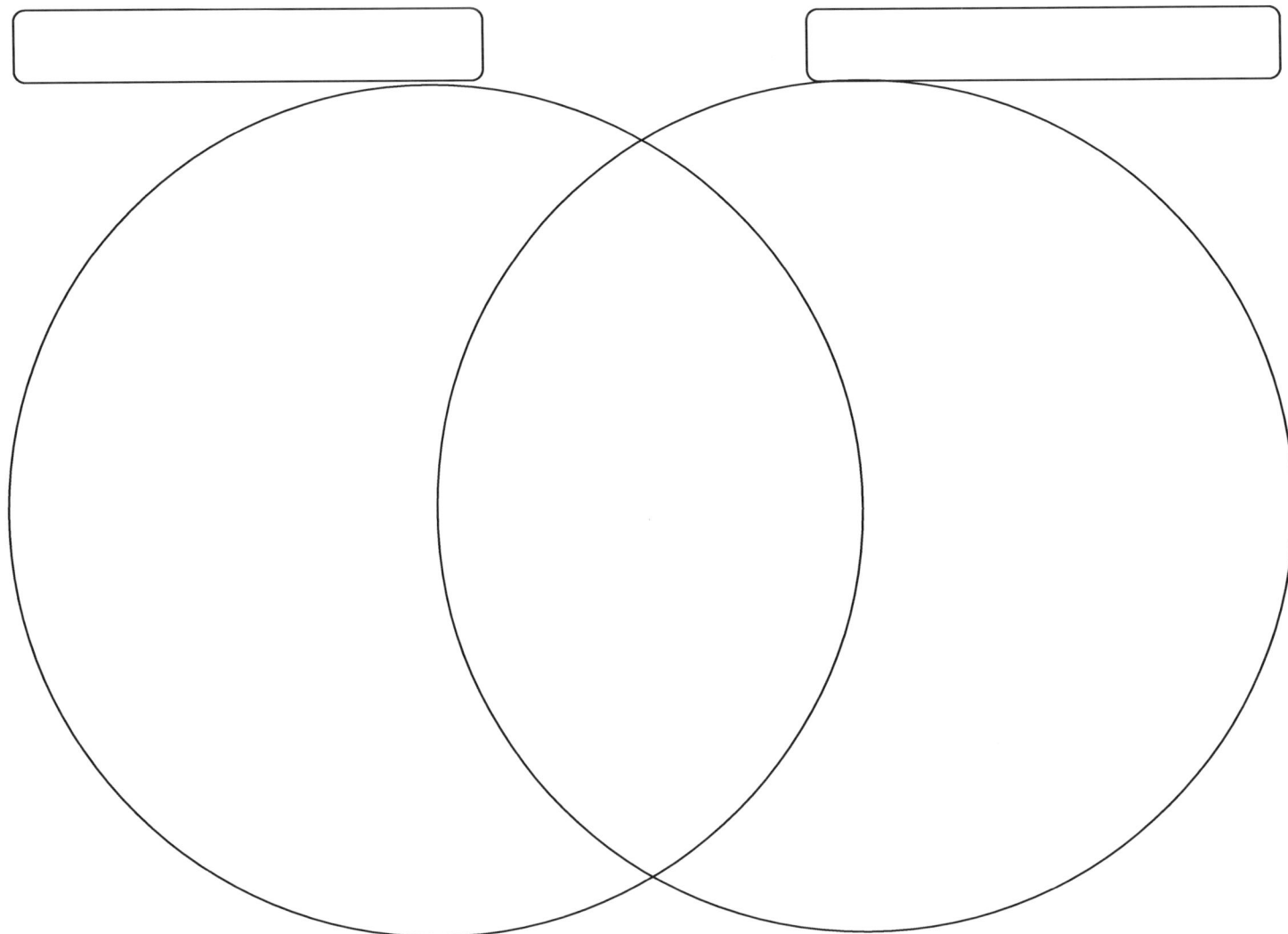

Create the Test

Question:

Answer:

Question:

Answer:

Question:

Answer:

Question:

Answer:

NAME:

TEACHER:

Date:

Draw the Scene: What five things have you included in the scene?

1   2   3

4   5

NAME:

TEACHER:

Date:

Interview: Who _____

Question:

Answer:

Question:

Answer:

Question:

Answer:

Question:

Answer:

NAME:

TEACHER:

Date:

Lost Scene: Write a scene that takes place between ________________________ and __________________________

Making Connections

What is the connection?

NAME:

TEACHER:

Date:

Precognition Sheet

Who ?

What's going to happen?

What will be the result?

Who ?

What's going to happen?

What will be the result?

Who ?

What's going to happen?

What will be the result?

Who ?

What's going to happen?

What will be the result?

How many did you get correct?

NAME:

TEACHER:

Date:

Assignment: Pyramid

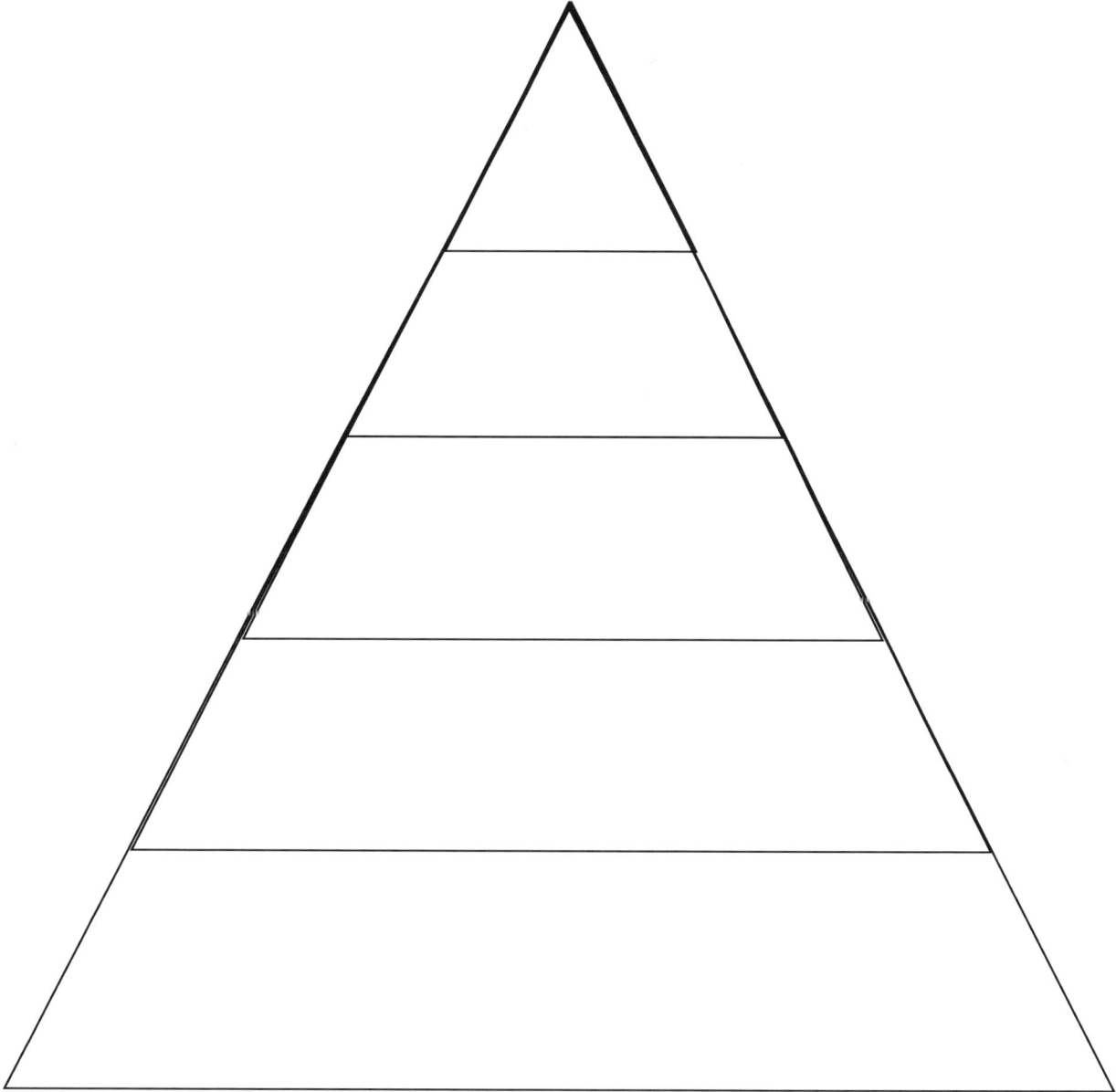

NAME:

TEACHER:

Date:

Research connections

What am I researching?

Source (URL, Book, Magazine, Interview)

Facts I found that could be useful or notes

1.

2.

3.

4.

5.

6.

1.

2.

3.

4.

5.

Sequencing or timeline

NAME:

TEACHER:

Date:

Support This!

Supporting text

What page?

Supporting text

What page?

Central idea or statement

Supporting text

What page?

Supporting text

What page?

Travel Brochure

Why should you visit?

What are you going to see?

Map

Special Events

Top Ten List

1.

2.

3.

4.

5.

6.

7.

8.

9.

10.

Vocabulary Box

Definition:

Draw:

Word:

Related words:

Use in a sentence:

Definition:

Draw:

Word:

Related words:

Use in a sentence:

NAME:

TEACHER:

Date:

What would you do?

Character: _____

What did they do?

Example from text:

What would you do?

Why would that be better?

Character: _____

What did they do?

Example from text:

What would you do?

Why would that be better?

Character: _____

What did they do?

Example from text:

What would you do?

Why would that be better?

NAME:

TEACHER:

Date:

Who, What, When, Where, and How

Who

What

Where

When

How

NAME:

TEACHER:

Date:

Write a letter

To:

From:

NAME:

TEACHER:

Date:

Assignment:

NAME:

TEACHER:

Date:

Add a Character

Who is the new character?

What reason does the new character have for being there?

Write a dialog between the new character and characters currently in the scene.

You dialog must be 6 lines or more, and can occur in the beginning, middle or end of the scene.

Costume Design

Draw a costume for one the characters in the scene.

Why do you believe this character should have a costume like this?

NAME:

TEACHER:

Date:

Props Needed

Prop:

What text from the scene supports this?

Prop:

What text from the scene supports this?

Prop:

What text from the scene supports this?

NAME:

TEACHER:

Date:

Soundtrack!

Song:

Why should this song be used?

Song:

Why should this song be used?

Song:

Why should this song be used?

NAME:

TEACHER:

Date:

Stage Directions

List who is moving, how they are moving and use text from the dialog to determine when they move.

Who:

How:

When:

Who:

How:

When:

Who:

How:

When:

NAME:

TEACHER:

Poetry Analysis

Date:

Name of Poem:

Subject:

Text Support:

Plot:

Text Support:

Theme:

Text Support:

Setting:

Text Support:

Tone:

Text Support:

Important Words and Phrases:

Why are these words and phrases important:

Made in the USA
Las Vegas, NV
20 June 2023

73658605R00057